MAKING
Classic
WEDDING
DRESSES

NICHOLAS BULLEN

Bell & Hyman
London

GRANDISON

First published in 1981 by
BELL & HYMAN LIMITED
Denmark House
37-39 Queen Elizabeth Street
London SE1 2QB
© Nicholas Bullen 1981
Designed by Richard Brown Associates

British Library Cataloguing in Publication Data
Bullen, Nicholas
Making classic wedding dresses.
1. Wedding costume   2. Sewing
I. Title
646.4'7   TT560
ISBN 0 7135 1283 0
Printed in Great Britain by Thomson Litho Limited,
East Kilbride
and bound by Hunter & Foulis, Edinburgh
for the publishers Bell & Hyman Limited

Contents

Introduction

However much the social and economic structure may change over the years the 'white wedding' ritual remains relatively unchanged since Victorian times. Before 1800 most wedding dresses were just the best dress the bride could afford, and were not necessarily white. They were usually similar in style to the evening dress of the period. Ever since the advent of the white wedding, brides from every social strata have sought to make it the most important and glamorous day of their lives.

These days the cost of a special white wedding dress has soared to many hundreds of pounds and many brides have tended to opt for a more casual and practical dress. However, my experience of designing wedding dresses over the past few years has shown that there is still a great demand for that individual dress for the big day. With this in mind I have researched every period of history, designing a range of wedding dresses based on the styles of dress from 1260 to 1920. The wedding dresses in this book have captured the romantic flavour of each period in designs suited to modern dress-making techniques.

White is, of course, the most obvious colour choice, but variations of subtle colours or patterned fabrics will make the dresses even more individual. The use of different colours is also more practical as they will then adapt to pretty and romantic evening dresses. It seems a shame that so much effort should go into a dress that is only to be worn once, so many of the designs can be used as evening dresses also. Individual taste will determine the choice of fabric or combination of fabrics used.

Each design is accompanied by a full set of quarter scale patterns to be found on the inserted sheets. A grid should be drawn up four times the size of the squares on the diagrams and the patterns can then be transferred to full scale. The patterns are designed for a size 12, but they can be altered easily to suit the individual's requirements. The shapes themselves have been kept as simple as possible so that the more complicated technicalities of pattern drafting can be avoided giving confidence to those not accustomed to using their own patterns. The garments should fulfill the exact requirements by their individual use of fabrics and trimmings, for that special day.

Basic Sewing Guidelines

So many potentially good dressmakers often forget how important the most basic procedures are to the look of the finished garment. The following hints might be useful:

Needles

Change the needle in your sewing machine frequently, since a blunt needle can badly damage a delicate fabric. Machines stitch incorrectly, not because the machine is at fault, but because the needle is the wrong size for the fabric type.

Use the following as a guide to the needle size:

1. Size 70/9 or 80/11 — light fabrics, e.g. chiffon, taffeta, voile, muslin, silk, crepe de Chine, lace.
2. Size 90/14 — medium fabrics, e.g. satin, moiré, slub silk, broderie anglaise, cotton.
3. Size 100/16 — heavy fabrics, e.g. velvet, brocade, Ottoman, damask.

Pressing

Press every seam as it is worked, *do not leave it until later*. Use a dry iron and the 'fingertip' method when pressing heavy fabrics, i.e. dip the fingertips in water and lightly dampen the stitching line in front of the iron. This method keeps only the seam area in contact with the moisture and leaves the rest of the garment free. For larger areas of heavy fabric use a fine damp cloth, well wrung. The flatter the seams, the more professional the look of the finished garment.

Trimming

To ensure a flat seam, it is important to get rid of any excess fabric during the making up. If a curve is stitched it must be clipped before pressing, i.e. the convex edge should have small 'V's cut from the seam allowance, whilst the concave edge should have small cuts into the seam allowance around the curve so that it spreads out when pressed flat. For curved neck edges cut the seam allowance to 5 mm ($\frac{1}{4}$ in) and, if exposed, bind with seam binding or machine zigzag the edge.

The term 'bagging out' applies to double areas such as the collar and cuffs where two pieces of fabric have the same shape and size and are seamed round the edge. This term can also apply to larger areas of the garment that are the same shape, e.g. a bodice can be bagged out on to the lining. The most important thing to remember when bagging out is that there should always be an opening to pull the fabric to the right side, thereby enclosing the seam allowance.

Sink stitching refers to a line of topstitching hidden in an already made-up seam.

Linings

For fine fabrics (see Needles above) use a Jap silk or the lightest rayon crepe de Chine. Medium fabrics should be lined with rayon taffeta or bemburg (a silky but firm lining) and heavy fabrics need a heavy satin or poult.

Threads

It is also very important to choose the correct thread for the job. When sewing with silk you must use a pure silk thread, sheer fabrics need a fine polyester thread and medium to heavy fabrics must be made up using a cotton thread.

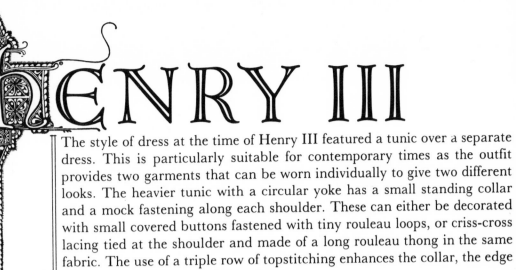

ḢENRY III

(1260)

The style of dress at the time of Henry III featured a tunic over a separate dress. This is particularly suitable for contemporary times as the outfit provides two garments that can be worn individually to give two different looks. The heavier tunic with a circular yoke has a small standing collar and a mock fastening along each shoulder. These can either be decorated with small covered buttons fastened with tiny rouleau loops, or criss-cross lacing tied at the shoulder and made of a long rouleau thong in the same fabric. The use of a triple row of topstitching enhances the collar, the edge of the yoke and the curved side slit hem.

The diaphanous underdress has a simple 'peasant' shape with an elasticated neck. The dress can be worn off the shoulder or slightly higher, just on the shoulder. The waist of the underdress is also elasticated and, if desired, a plaited rouleau sash can be worn over the tunic.

A matching rouleau circlet would make an attractive headdress with an optional veil, a rectangle of fine cloth gathered on to the band. The bridesmaids could be dressed in the underdress made in a coloured or printed voile.

Suggested fabrics
Tunic: raw silk, Thai silk, silk twill, brocade, Ottoman, velvet, moiré. (If using any of the last four fabrics, buy silk cords instead of making rouleaux as the fabric is too thick.)

Underdress: plain or printed chiffon, Swiss voile, organdie, silk crepe de Chine, silk jersey.

Approximate fabric requirement for size 12
Tunic: 3 m ($3\frac{1}{4}$ yd).
Underdress: 6 m ($6\frac{1}{2}$ yd).

Notions:
One 55 cm ($21\frac{3}{4}$ in) zipper, seam binding, small pearl or fabric-covered buttons and rouleau loops *or* small eyelets and silk cords, 140 cm (55 in) narrow elastic, sewing thread.

Construction
Tunic
1. Having drafted the pattern to full scale, cut also facing patterns for the edge of the yoke, the armhole and the hem. These are denoted by dotted lines.

2. Add a 3 cm ($1\frac{1}{2}$ in) seam allowance down the centre back of the yoke and body for the zipper.

3. Add a 1.5 cm ($\frac{5}{8}$ in) seam allowance on to all other edges.

4. Extend the shoulder seams for 4 cm ($1\frac{1}{8}$ in). If loops and buttons are used fold the front extension so that the back lies underneath the front. If the shoulders are to be laced, fold both edges underneath

5. Cut out all pieces and finish off the side seams, centre back seams, yoke seam and the inside edges of the facings by zigzagging or binding with bias. The method used to finish the edges is determined by the thickness of fabric used.

6. Stitch the centre back seam to the point where the zipper is inserted. Press seam open along the entire length of centre back.

7. Stitch bust darts and press downwards.

8. Stitch side seams and press open.

9. Stitch side seams of armhole facings.

10. Stitch the facings on to the garment, right sides together, clip the curves and press to the inside.

11. Stitch centre back seam and side seams of the hem facing and repeat stage 10, clipping right into the notch on the pattern where the split starts.

12. Work three rows of topstitching 3 mm ($\frac{1}{8}$ in) apart all the way round the hem to emphasize the shape and to secure the facing firmly on the inside.

13. Stitch the front and back facings to the yoke, right sides together. The type of fastening required will determine whether to bag the facing out with the shoulder extension (for an underlap) or whether to cut it short so that the extension can fold inside and meet the opposite facing (for edge to edge). The alternative seam lines are shown by the dotted lines.

14. Fold in the centre back seam allowance of the yoke and stitch it to the facing.

15. Clip the curved seam allowances of the yoke facings and press to the inside. Lay the yoke on top of the front and back panels of the underdress, matching the notches on the yoke panels with the dress. Now topstitch as for the hem (see stage 12).

16. The yoke is in three pieces, so the triple rows of topstitching should continue from the curve of the yokes up along the shoulder line.

17. Now attach the mock fastenings to the shoulders. If a button fastening is required affix small rouleau loops under the front edge and sew small pearl or fabric-covered buttons to the back edge. Alternatively, if a laced fastening is required make small eyelets along each side of the shoulder and lace together with long silk cords.

18. Having cut out the collar on the bias, bag out the centre back ends and topstitch as for other edges (see stage 12). If a quilted effect is desired, a thin layer of wadding may be put inside.

19. Stitch the collar to the neck making sure that both shoulders are edge to edge and that the centre back zipper allowance of the yoke is turned to the outside, thus sandwiching the collar between the yoke and the zipper facing.

20. Clip seam allowances and press the yoke downwards.

21. Finally insert the zipper, preferably by hand, from the top of the collar down through the yoke to the notch shown on the pattern.

Underdress

1. Draft the pattern to full scale and lengthen the skirt from the waist to the hem to the required length.

2. Add a 1 cm ($\frac{3}{8}$ in) seam allowance to every edge except the centre back and centre front which are on the fold.

3. Cut out the four pattern pieces allowing 2 cm ($\frac{7}{8}$ in) for the hem.

4. Stitch the side seams, finishing with a 5 mm ($\frac{1}{4}$ in) French seam.

5. Stitch the underarm seam of the sleeve, finishing with a 5 mm ($\frac{1}{4}$ in) French seam.

6. Stitch the raglan sleeve into the armhole matching the notches and the seams and finishing with a French seam as above.

7. Work a row of tight machine stitches 1 cm ($\frac{3}{8}$ in) from the neck edge to retain the shape.

8. Stitch a narrow seam binding in the colour of the fabric to the outside edge of the neck and hem of the sleeves.

9. Press binding to the inside of the garment and edgestitch to create a channel for narrow elastic.

10. Thread 64 cm ($25\frac{1}{4}$ in) of narrow elastic through the neck. This will give a round loose neckline and also one that can be pulled down over the shoulders for a 'barer' look.

11. Thread 16 cm ($6\frac{1}{4}$ in) of narrow elastic through each cuff.

12. Mark the waistline with tailors' chalk and edgestitch a channel of the seam binding to the inside of the dress along this line.

13. Thread 60 cm ($23\frac{3}{4}$ in) of narrow elastic through the waist.

The underdress is now complete. It is a very simple and practical garment that starts as an underdress for a wedding and can later be used as a pretty and provocative evening dress. If a less sheer effect is desired use fine silk lining for the main body of the dress and make up as a separate underdress, only attached at the neck and armholes.

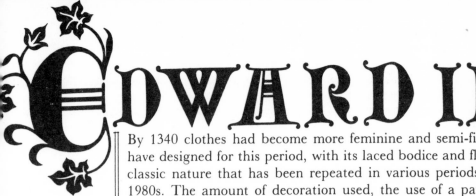

EDWARD III

(1340)

By 1340 clothes had become more feminine and semi-fitted. The style I have designed for this period, with its laced bodice and flared skirt, is of a classic nature that has been repeated in various periods right up to the 1980s. The amount of decoration used, the use of a patterned fabric or braid trim, is up to the individual. Without the long, slashed oversleeves and made in a richer or brighter fabric, this dress would make a simple but effective evening dress.

The fitted high-waisted bodice with its wide circular neckline has a border sewn on as an outside facing of patterned braid. The open front is laced together with a rouleau thong of the same fabric. A silk cord with tassels at each end would make a good alternative. The narrow straight sleeves are bordered in the same way as the neckline and the full-length oversleeves are open to show a contrast pattern. If the dress itself is made of a self-patterned fabric use a plain material for the borders and oversleeve lining. The skirt is made in four panels and is fitted at the top, flaring to a bordered hem.

With the long sleeves a veil seems unnecessary. A plain circlet of braid, pearls or flowers would be fine for the headdress. Dress the bridesmaids in the same style, either in a plain colour or in flower-printed fabric with a plain contrast trim.

Suggested fabrics

Dress: plain heavy silk, velvet, damask, brocade, taffeta.
Trim: patterned silk crepe de Chine, moiré, decorated braid.
Lining: heavy satin, poult.

Approximate fabric requirement for a size 12

Dress: 5.5 m (6 yd).
Trim (including sleeve lining): 2.5 m ($2\frac{3}{4}$ yd).

Notions

One 55 cm ($21\frac{3}{4}$ in) zipper, eight small metal eyelets, silk cord, four silk tassels, interfacing, boning (optional), sewing thread

Construction

Dress

1. Draft the pattern to full scale and add a 1.5 cm ($\frac{5}{8}$ in) seam allowance to all edges except the centre back. This edge should have a 3 cm ($1\frac{1}{8}$ in) seam allowance for the 55 cm ($21\frac{3}{4}$ in) zipper.

15

2. Trace off all the sections of the border on the bodice front, back, undersleeve, skirt hem and sleeve border.

3. Join the back and front bodice pieces at the darts, where the notches are marked on the pattern.

4. Add a 1 cm ($\frac{3}{8}$ in) seam allowance to all inside edges of these borders including the mitred corners on the front opening of the bodice.

5. Cut out all the borders and lining of the oversleeve in the contrast fabric.

6. Stitch the bust dart, shoulder dart and back dart of the bodice.

7. Stitch the side seams and shoulder seams. Press open.

8. Repeat stages 6 and 7 for the bodice lining.

9. Place the bodice on to the lining so that all the seam allowances are sandwiched between the two layers and are hence invisible.

10. If the contrast fabric is quite fine interface the border pieces to stiffen them.

11. Stitch all side seams, front mitres and shoulder seams. Press all these seams open to give one continuous edging.

12. Machine a line of small stitches 1 cm ($\frac{3}{8}$ in) in all round the inner edge of the neck. This will keep the neckline in shape during the next stage.

13. Place the border on the ironing board, right side down, and carefully press the 1 cm ($\frac{3}{8}$ in) seam allowance towards you using the stitching line as a guide. (The stitching should be just on the inside so that it is invisible from the right side.) To ensure a good flat edge wet your fingertips and run them along the seam allowance as you fold it out in front of the tip of the iron.

14. Tack the border with the right side facing the inside of the bodice, round the neck and centre fronts. Make sure that the shoulder seams match.

15. Machine the three thicknesses together 1.5 cm ($\frac{5}{8}$ in) in from the outside edge. Trim the seam allowance of the actual dress fabric down to 5 mm ($\frac{1}{4}$ in) to reduce the bulk.

16. Trim the corners on the centre front and clip the seam allowances on the neck curves.

17. Press the border out on to the outside of the bodice using the method described in stage 13.

18. Place the border flat on to the bodice so that the pressed in edge is exactly parallel to the outside edge. Match side seams along the bottom edge and at the shoulder seams. Tack in position.

19. Edgestitch the border down to the bodice following the very edge of the pressed in seam allowance.

20. Press in the 3 cm ($1\frac{1}{8}$ in) centre back seam allowance.

21. Insert small metal eyelets down either side of the centre front as marked on the pattern.

22. If such a low neckline is not desired, hand sew some tape down the lower half of the front bodice on the inside so that it invisibly joins the centre together. From the outside, however, this will still give the impression of an opening that goes right down to the skirt seam.

23. If the fabric of the garment is not substantial enough, it would be wise to insert boning to the insides of the centre front.

24. Make up two sleeves in dress fabric and two in lining. Mount the lining with no seam allowances showing and tack around the sleeve head and along the hem. Join the side seams of the border and press the top edge in. Stitch to the inside of the sleeve, press to the right side and edgestitch down.

25. For the oversleeve cut two in dress fabric and two in the contrast border fabric.

26. Bag the two sets out so that you have a pair of oversleeves with the dress fabric facing the dress and the contrast facing the outside. Tack round the armholes in this position, matching the notches and making the two top points meet at the shoulder seam.

27. Tack in the undersleeves, again matching the notches.

28. Stitch through all thicknesses, 1.5 cm ($\frac{5}{8}$ in) in. Trim to 5 mm ($\frac{1}{4}$ in) and finish the edges with seam binding or by zigzagging the seam allowances together. (The method used depends on the thickness of the fabric.)

29. The upper edges of the oversleeve can be turned back along the dotted line of the pattern to reveal the contrast fabric.

30. Stitch the four panels of the skirt together and press the seam allowances open. Remember that the 3 cm ($1\frac{1}{8}$ in) centre back seam should finish at the notch marked on the pattern, so that the zipper can be inserted.

31. Repeat stage 30 for the skirt lining and tack both lining and skirt together at the top so that the seam allowances are facing each other and are, therefore, invisible.

32. Machine the skirt to the bodice and finish the seam allowances using binding or zigzagging.

33. Insert the centre back zipper by hand stab stitching.

34. Stitch the hem border pieces together and repeat stage 24. It is important to keep the lining separate from the skirt round the hem. Finish hem lining separately.

35. Lace up the centre front with silk cord and finish with silk tassels at each end of the cord and at the points of the oversleeves.

Richard II

(1430)

The longer, leaner bodice silhouette with the gathered skirt typical of this period make for a more formal and grand wedding dress, suitably in white.

The hip-length bodice is like a fitted jacket with the edges round the inset front panel piped. The long tight-fitting sleeves have a flared cuff and piped edge with a covered button and loop fastening up to the elbow. The full skirt is flared and gathered on to the hip. There are fewer gathers at the front, becoming very full at the back and falling into a train. To achieve the maximum effect it is best to use a heavy self-patterned fabric for the bodice and if desired use a contrasting scale pattern for the centre front panel. Alternatively, use self-pattern for the front panel and a plain fabric for the rest, giving the effect of a jacket over a bodice. The skirt should be of a lighter fabric so that it gathers neatly on the hip and flows out into the hem and train.

The headdress is made from a purchased white velvet wired Alice band. This is then wound with pearls and a short or long silk tulle veil gathered into it. A plastic hair comb sewn to the headdress will keep it secure. The bridesmaids could wear a similar dress to the bride, but with no train, plain coloured bodices and patterned voile skirts.

Suggested fabrics
Bodice: brocade, velvet, figured crepe de Chine, taffeta, satin.
Skirt: plain crepe de Chine, chiffon, voile, organdie, georgette, crepe.
Lining: heavy satin, poult.

Approximate fabric requirement for size 12
Bodice: 3 m ($3\frac{1}{4}$ yd).
Skirt: 7 m ($7\frac{1}{2}$ yd).
Lining: 10 m (11 yd).

Notions
One 50 cm (20 in) zipper, piping cord, rouleau loops, six covered buttons, sewing thread.

Construction
1. Draft the pattern to full scale and add a 1.5 cm ($\frac{5}{8}$ in) seam allowance to all seams except the centre back seam which has a 3 cm ($1\frac{1}{8}$ in) seam to allow for the zipper.

2. Cut out the pattern pieces in the chosen fabrics of the dress plus an exact duplicate in lining fabric.

3. Mount all nine pieces of the bodice on to the lining, tacking the two together right round the seam allowances.

4. Stitch the shoulder darts and the shoulder seams. Press open.

5. Cut strips of silk, 3 cm ($1\frac{1}{8}$ in) wide on the bias to use as piping on the bodice seams. The length required is approximately 110 cm ($43\frac{1}{2}$ in) not all in one piece. Use the seams on the bodice for a more accurate measurement.

6. To make the piping, fold the strips in half and using the zipper foot sandwich the piping cord inside the fabric, stitching as close as possible to the enclosed cord.

7. Still using the zipper foot stitch the piping to the bust panels and the back panels so that the seam allowances are all edge to edge with the piping facing in towards the middle of the pattern pieces.

8. Stitch the two sets of back panels together and the two sets of front panels with the piping sandwiched in between. Press seams open carefully.

9. Stitch the side seams and press open. You should now have a sleeveless 'jacket', open at the back and front.

10. Stitch piping across the top of the centre front panel and press the seam allowance down to the inside. Since the piping is on the bias there is no need to finish off the edge. However, it might be advisable to catch down the seam allowance to the lining, just to make sure that it is secure. Repeat this procedure for the curved base of this panel.

11. Stitch the piping all the way round the outer edge of the sleeveless 'jacket', from the top centre back to the lower centre back line. Press and secure as in stage 10.

12. Lay the centre front panel under the two piped edges of the 'jacket' front so that the piping overlaps for the 1.5 cm ($\frac{5}{8}$ in) seam allowance. The notches on the pattern show the exact position.

13. Using the zipper foot again work a row of sink stitching as close to the piping as possible so that the front panel is attached to the rest of the bodice (the piping should hide this topstitching).

14. Stitch the sleeve seams to the notch shown on the pattern. Press seams open.

15. Repeat stage 14 for the lining.

16. With the sleeves right sides out and using the zipper foot, stitch piping to the right side of the cuffs.

17. Slip the lining over the top with the seam allowances outside. Tack round the bottom and machine from the inside following the exact line of the stitching as in stage 16.

18. Turn the sleeve lining up into the inside of the sleeve and press the bottom of the cuff so that the piping is right on the edge.

19. Hand stitch the lining to the cuff opening, sandwiching in rouleau loops which will fasten over small covered buttons.

20. Stitch the sleeves into the bodice and then hand stitch the sleeve lining to the armhole.

21. Stitch the five panels of the skirt (if fabric is sheer use French seams) and press seams open. Repeat for the lining.

22. Mount the skirt on to the lining and run a double gathering stitch along the top.

23. Lay the bodice over the gathered skirt at the waistband, adjusting the fullness so that the centre back, side seams and the bodice seams all match. This should mean that the skirt is flat at the front, becoming increasingly full round to the train at the back.

24. Tuck in place and sink stitch through to beside the piping as in stage 13.

25. Hand stitch the zipper into the bodice and sew on covered buttons to give the impression of being fastened with buttons and loops.

26. Stitch the two hems separately, making each as shallow as possible as the hemline is shaped into the train.

REFORMATION

(1500)

Although this dress is not typical of that worn in England at the time of Henry VII it is similar to those being drawn by Dürer in Germany at that time. Obviously an adaptation, I feel that it is stylish and appropriate enough to be worn at either a church or register office wedding, becoming a stunning outfit for evening wear.

Although rather elaborate in appearance this top and skirt relies on the beauty of finely pleated sheer fabric to provide its elegance. It is possible to purchase ready-pleated fabric, but few people seem to realize that it is quite inexpensive to have fabric of one's own choice pleated by professional pleaters. This gives the individual an endless variety of colour and choice of fabric, although generally the finer the fabric the more effective the resulting garment. For example, if using white chiffon, a pastel coloured lining would be very pretty, but a more sensational result could be achieved by using a pale tone of chiffon over a deeper shade of silk, used also for the yoke and cuffs.

The outfit consists of a tunic top with deep pointed yoke and centre front buttoning up to a high collar. This collar can be folded down for a more casual look. The full pleated sleeves are gathered into cuffs made to match the yoke. The waist can be elasticated and topped by a silk belt. The long narrow skirt is elasticated at the waist and fluted out at the hem.

A suitable headdress for this outfit would be a purchased pillbox trimmed with pearls and secured at the back of the head with a plastic hair comb. Dress the bridesmaids in a fairly simple style made up in a plain coloured fabric.

Suggested fabrics

Pleating: chiffon, georgette, voile, crepe de Chine (Fabric to be pleated must not be less than 115 cm [44/45 in] wide.)
Yoke: silk crepe de Chine, silk taffeta, silk twill.
Lining: Jap silk, rayon crepe de Chine.

Approximate fabric requirement for a size 12

Pleating: 5 m ($5\frac{1}{2}$ yd) pleated fabric, or 15 m (16 yd) fabric to be pleated. (Ask for flat pleats straight.)
Yoke, collar and cuffs: 2 m ($2\frac{1}{4}$ yd).
Lining: 5 m ($5\frac{1}{2}$ yd).

Notions

One 20 cm (8 in) zipper (see skirt, stage 2), small fabric-covered buttons and rouleau loops, binding tape, 120 cm (48 in) narrow elastic, sewing thread.

Construction

Pleated top with plain yoke, cuffs and tie belt

1. Draft the pattern to full scale adding a 3 cm ($1\frac{1}{8}$ in) seam allowance to the centre back seam and a 1 cm ($\frac{3}{8}$ in) seam allowance to all other edges. Cut out the yokes, collar and cuffs in plain fabric.

2. If a self sash is required, cut a band in the same fabric 3 m x 6 cm (118 in x $2\frac{3}{8}$ in). These measurements include a 1 cm ($\frac{3}{8}$ in) seam allowance on each side.

3. Pin the pleated fabric with the pleats closed on a flat surface. Lay the pattern pieces down on the fabric, weight them and chalk round the edge (not including the seam allowance).

4. Remove the paper patterns and tack all the way round the chalked edges before cutting out. Add the 1.5 cm ($\frac{5}{8}$ in) seam allowance.

5. Machine round the tacked edges to keep the pleats in place.

6. Stitch the two separate front yokes to the two separate back yokes along the shoulder seams. Press open.

7. Stitch the collar to the two yokes, clip the neck seam allowances and press open.

8. Bag out around the top collar edge and the bottom yoke edge with right sides together. Turn out and press, leaving the centre front edges open.

9. Press in the centre front edges to the seam allowance so that they are edge to edge.

10. Make 5 mm ($\frac{1}{4}$ in) rouleau loops and attach them to one edge of the centre front.

11. Hand stitch the two edges of the centre front together so that one edge falls slightly inside the other.

12. Stitch fabric-covered buttons to the very edge of the centre front opposite the rouleau loop edge. The yoke is now complete.

13. Stitch the front edge of the sleeve to the front edge of the bodice armhole. Finish the seam by cutting to 5 mm ($\frac{1}{4}$ in) and zigzagging.

14. Repeat stage 13 for the back sleeves.

15. Match the centre fronts, armhole notches and centre back marks. Lay the yoke on top of the pleated bodice with the centre fronts of the yoke edge to edge. Tack in position along the machined line of the pleating and edgestitch the yoke on to the bodice.

16. Mark the waistline of the back and front of the pleated bodice with tailors' chalk. Machine a narrow tape or ribbon (in a matching colour) to the inside to give a channel for the elastic. Remember to finish the tape 1.5 cm ($\frac{5}{8}$ in) in from the side seams so that it does not get caught up here.

17. Stitch the side seams of the bodice and sleeves in one line of stitiching, carefully matching the underarm points A and B. Finish as in stage 13.

18. Thread 60 cm ($23\frac{3}{4}$ in) of narrow elastic through the tape using a hairgrip. Fasten off the ends.

19. Gather the pleated edge of the sleeve into the top edge of the cuff with a wide gathering stitch.

20. Attach rouleau loops as for the centre front, fold the cuff right sides together and bag out the ends.

21. Turn back to the inside, press and hand stitch the inside edge of the cuff to the sleeve.

22. Stitch fabric-covered buttons on to the opposite edge of the rouleau loops.

23. Finish off the hem of the tunic with a machine-rolled edge, flattening the pleats so that the hem flutes out.

Skirt

1. If the fabric is wide enough for a full-length skirt use the following method:
   (a) Stitch the side seams, trimming down to 5 mm ($\frac{1}{4}$ in) and zigzagging together the seam allowances.
   (b) Cut the flat lining to the skirt using the measurements for the closed pleat pattern. Attach the lining to the waist seam.
   (c) Stitch a channel of tape to the waist and thread in 60 cm ($23\frac{3}{4}$ in) of narrow elastic as in stage 18.
   (d) Finish the hem as in stage 23.

2. However, if the fabric is too narrow and a hip yoke is required use the following method:
   (a) Cut out the three yoke pieces, adding a 1.5 cm ($\frac{5}{8}$ in) seam allowance on waist, side and hip edges and a 3 cm ($1\frac{1}{8}$ in) seam allowance on the centre back seam to allow for the 20 cm (8 in) zipper. The yoke will be covered by the tunic top.
   (b) Cut out the yoke in plain fabric, stitch the side seams and press open. Bind the waistline with tape and press to the inside.
   (c) Stitch the two pleated panels as for stages 1(a) and (b) for the lining.
   (d) Attach pleated skirt and lining to hip line of the yoke and finish off by binding the edges.
   (e) Sew in zipper by hand.
   (f) Finish the hem as in stage 23.

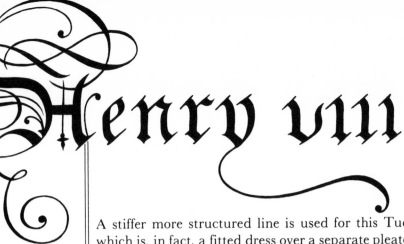

Henry viii

(1530)

A stiffer more structured line is used for this Tudor-style wedding dress which is, in fact, a fitted dress over a separate pleated chiffon blouse. Either can be worn afterwards for evening wear — the dress on its own for more formal occasions and the blouse with a long skirt or trousers for a more casual look.

The dress is made of six panels, fitted on the bodice and then flared out to a full hem, cut slightly longer at the back to give a slight train. The square neck, the hems of the wide trumpet-shaped sleeves and the skirt are all edged with a contrast band, preferably of white velvet. This gives the style lines extra emphasis and firmness and is especially effective as a matt contrast to the shiny white silk or satin, the most suitable fabric for the main body of the dress. However, an equally stunning effect would be achieved by using a very pale oyster, cream or ice pink for the dress and this would then be more useful for evening wear later. The pleated chiffon blouse has a simple tunic shape with very full sleeves and the round neck gathered into a rouleau binding. As mentioned in the previous chapter, pleated fabric may be bought ready-made or fabric of the individual's choice professionally pleated.

Tudor-style headdresses can be purchased in bridal departments of large stores and a short or floor-length veil gathered on at the back. The bridesmaids could wear the same style in a self-patterned fabric but without the blouse underneath.

Suggested fabrics
Dress: velvet, satin, heavy silk, damask, brocade, Ottoman, moiré.
Blouse: pleated chiffon.
Lining: heavy satin, poult.

Approximate fabric requirement for a size 12

Dress: 8 m (8¾ yd).
Blouse: 3 m (3¼ yd) pleated fabric, or 9 m (9¾ yd) fabric to be pleated.
Lining: 8 m (8¾ yd).

Notions
One 50 cm (20 in) zipper, 2.5 m (2¾ yd) white velvet ribbon, sewing thread.

Construction

Dress

1. Draft the pattern to full scale and add a 1.5 cm ($\frac{5}{8}$ in) seam allowance to all the dress panel edges, a 3 cm ($1\frac{1}{8}$ in) seam allowance to the centre back (including the yoke) to allow for the zipper, and a 1 cm ($\frac{3}{8}$ in) seam allowance to all other edges. Cut out the pattern pieces in fabric and lining making sure to cut separate patterns for the hem edgings and sleeve edgings. The linings should be cut right down to the bottom of the hem.

2. Stitch the contrast edges on to the hem panels of the skirt and to the hems of the sleeves by mounting them on top of the actual fabric. This will give added stiffness.

3. Stitch all the seams of the dress panels, making sure that all the contrast hem edges match perfectly. Press seams open.

4. Stitch the centre back seam to the notch marked for the zipper. Press seam open.

5. Stitch the front yoke to the front dress panels and press seams downwards.

6. Repeat stage 5 for the back yokes.

7. Stitch shoulder seams of the yoke and press open.

8. Stitch all the dress panel seams of the lining and press open.

9. Stitch front and back inner fabric yokes to the linings and press seams downwards.

10. Repeat stage 7.

11. Lay the dress lining on top of the dress with the right sides together. Tack round the square neck of the yokes.

12. Machine right the way round the neck, double stitching the corners to give added strength.

13. Clip the corners and turn the lining to the inside. Press.

14. Tack the armhole linings to the dress armholes.

15. Hand stitch the zipper into the back of the dress. Turn the centre back seam allowances of the lining to the inside and hand stitch the folded edge of the lining 5 mm ($\frac{1}{4}$ in) away from the zipper teeth.

16. Press a hem of 1 cm ($\frac{3}{8}$ in) on both the dress and the lining.

17. Hand stitch the two hems together so that the seam allowances are sandwiched between the two. Make sure that the lining is 5 mm ($\frac{1}{4}$ in) shorter on the inside of the hem so that it does not show.

18. Stitch the sleeve seams in the fabric and lining and press open.

19. Lay the sleeve lining on top of the dress sleeve, right sides together. Tack round the hem and then machine, 1 cm ($\frac{3}{8}$ in) in.

20. Turn the lining inside the sleeve and press round the hem edge so that the lining points up into the sleeve.

21. Tack the sleeves into the armholes of the dress (not the linings) and machine in.

22. Finally, hand stitch the sleeve lining to the armhole of the dress on the inside.

Blouse
The chiffon blouse can be made in exactly the same way as for that in chapter 1, Henry III (1260), p. 9. If pleated chiffon is used, lay the pattern pieces flat on to the closed pleats, cut out and machine round the edges and stitch in the pleats, treating it like flat fabric.

ELIZABETH I

The height of Elizabethan fashion with the rigid padded bodices, stiff farthingale skirts and enormous sleeves, all heavily encrusted with jewels, does not readily lend itself to bridal wear in the 1980s. The style I propose for this period is a much softer one, embodying several Elizabethan features into a more romantic look. The advantage of the outfit is that it becomes a ravishing summer evening dress with a dramatic sleeveless coat to be worn perhaps over a black evening dress or a black blouse with a long black skirt or trousers.

The design consists of a delicate silk dress with a yoke and full sleeves in lace or spotted and flowered voile. The high neck and cuffs are hand or machine smocked with deep ruffles of fine lace. Worn over this is a floor-length sleeveless coat with cap shoulders, laced with silk thongs and a billowing flared hemline. For the best results use a heavy patterned damask or brocade.

The headdress is a ready-made snood, beaded with pearls and attached to a jewelled, wired Alice band. Dress the bridesmaids in dresses of a similar style made in flowered voile, but without the coat.

Suggested fabrics
Dress: lace, silk, spotted Swiss voile, flowered Swiss organza.
Coat: damask, brocade, moiré.
Lining: Jap silk, rayon de crepe de Chine.

Approximate fabric requirement for a size 12
Dress: 3 m (3½ yd) for the yoke, collar and sleeves. 5 m (5½ yd) for the main body.
Coat: 6 m (6½ yd).
Lining: 5 m (5½ yd) for the dress, 5 m (5½ yd) for the coat.

Notions
Lace edging, clear nylon press-studs or hooks and eyes, seam binding, metal eyelets, silk thong, frilled lace, sewing thread.

Construction

Dress
1. Draft the pattern to full scale and add a 1 cm (⅜ in) seam allowance to all edges.

2. Cut out the yoke, collar, sleeves and cuffs in lace only. Cut these pieces *twice* the size of the given pattern pieces to allow for contraction during smocking.

3. Cut out the main body in chosen fabric. Cut out the lining.

33

4. Stitch the main body of the dress, finishing the seams with 5 mm ($\frac{1}{4}$ in) French seams if the fabric is sheer.

5. Repeat stage 4 for the lining.

6. Tack the dress and lining together along the yoke seams and round the armholes.

7. Stitch the shoulder seams of the yoke using 5 mm ($\frac{1}{4}$ in) French seams.

8. Stitch the yoke to the dress, wrong sides together, so that the seam allowances come on the outside. Press the seam allowances downwards.

9. Cover the above seam allowances with a band of frilled lace, either topstitched down or hand sewn.

10. Either hand or machine smock the band for the collar. Then cut it to the right size and stitch it on to the neckline. Finish the seam on the inside either by binding or zigzagging.

11. The top edge of the collar can be trimmed with as many lace frills as desired.

12. Since a zipper would be too heavy use the following instructions for the centre back opening. Press one seam allowance in, underlapping the other. Fasten with tiny clear nylon press-studs or hooks and eyes, right up to the top of the collar.

13. Stitch the side seams of the sleeves using 5 mm ($\frac{1}{4}$ in) French seams.

14. The cuffs should be made following the instructions in stages 10 and 11.

15. Gather the sleeves into the cuffs and bind the seam allowances.

16. The hem can be machine rolled or, if using a very fine fabric, it should be rolled by hand.

Floor-length sleeveless coat
1. Draft the pattern to full scale and add a 1.5 cm ($\frac{5}{8}$ in) seam allowance to all edges. Cut out the pattern.

2. Cut out in fabric and in lining.

3. Stitch the coat sections together leaving shoulder seams open. Press seams open.

4. Repeat stage 3 for the lining.

5. Lay the lining on top of the waistcoat right sides together and tack round the edges, leaving the hem open.

6. Machine over your tacking and turn the lining to the inside. Press edges firmly. Use edgestitching to improve the edge.

7. Press the hems up inside to face each other. Either hand stitch together or machine edgestitch.

8. Insert eyelets into both sides of the shoulders where marked on the pattern.

9. Lace the shoulders together with silk thongs and finish ends with knots or tassels.

CHARLES I

(1635)

The romantic look of this period has rarely been revived, yet the lines and proportions are so graceful and sophisticated that the design is perfect for a grand wedding dress.

The bodice consists of a high-waisted jacket with fitted curved seams and a full peplum. The shawl collar is cut in silk like a folded head scarf and edged with deep frills of lace or broderie anglaise. These frills can be dotted with pearls for an even more luxurious look. The very full sleeves are gathered into the bodice and then into a deep cuff that is lace-trimmed to match the collar. The billowing skirt is flat at the front with soft pleats at the sides. These pleats become deeper towards the back of the skirt, falling into a graceful train.

The headdress is made from a purchased satin pillbox, trimmed with a triple row of pearls and with a long gathered silk tulle veil attached at the back. A concealed plastic hair comb will hold this in place. Dress the bridesmaids in a version of the same dress but without the shawl collar and with the V-neck edged with one row of lace. The bodice could be made in a plain coloured velvet with printed voile sleeves and skirt, giving the effect of a two-tone jacket and skirt. A plain circlet of mixed flowers would make a suitable headdress.

Suggested fabrics
Jacket and skirt: satin, velvet, silk, moiré, taffeta, damask, brocade.
Lining: heavy satin, poult.

Approximate fabric requirement for a size 12
Jacket and skirt: 8 m (8¾ yd) main fabric, 2 m (2¼ yd) contrasting fabric for collar and cuffs.
Lining: 8 m (8¾ yd).

Notions
One 20 cm (8 in) skirt zipper, pearly buttons, hooks and eyes, lace or broderie anglaise frills, interfacing, sewing thread.

Construction

Jacket
1. Draft the pattern to full scale and add a 1 cm ($\frac{5}{8}$ in) seam allowance to all seams. Except for the sleeves, duplicate all bodice pieces in lining fabric.

2. Stitch the curved seams of the front and back bodice and the side seams. Press open, clipping the curves to ensure that they lie flat.

3. Repeat stage 2 for the lining.

4. Iron on a band of interfacing 2 cm ($\frac{3}{4}$ in) wide down the centre front to reinforce the buttonholes.

5. Stitch the shoulder seams of both jacket and lining and press open.

6. Cut two silk collars on the bias, bag out around the outer edge and trim with various frills of lace or broderie anglaise.

7. Tack the collar round the neck edge, matching shoulder notches.

8. Place the bodice lining on top of the collar and bodice with the right sides sandwiched in.

9. Machine round the neck edge and down the centre front.

10. Trim the corners and clip the curves of the neck edge.

11. Turn the lining to the inside and press so that the collar stands up into a soft shawl effect.

12. Tack the lining to the bodice around the armhole and peplum seam.

13. Stitch the side seams of the peplum in both fabric and lining. Press seams open.

14. With right sides together machine round the outside edge of the peplum. Clip the curves and press the lining to the inside.

5. Carefully match the side seams and centre back notches and stitch the outer edge of the peplum to the outside of the bodice. Press the seams downwards.

16. Press the lining seam allowance of the peplum to the inside of the jacket and hand stitch to the lining of the bodice along the peplum seam.

17. Stitch the side seams of the jacket sleeve, press open and finish off the edges of the seam allowances by zigzagging.

18. Softly pleat the top of the sleeve into the armhole where marked on the patterm and stitch the sleeve into the jacket. Bind or zigzag the edges.

19. Make two separate cuffs by bagging out the sides and lower edges. Clip the corners and press the lining to the inside.

20. Softly pleat the base of the sleeve into the cuff and bind the inside seam allowances.

21. Trim the cuffs by adding lace ruffles (matching those of the collar). Sew these on by hand.

22. Fasten with small hand-worked loops and tiny pearl buttons.

Skirt

1. Draft the pattern to full scale and add a 1 cm ($\frac{3}{8}$ in) seam allowance to all seams except one side seam. Allow a 3 cm ($1\frac{1}{8}$ in) seam allowance on this edge to take a 20cm (8 in) skirt zipper.

2. Stitch all seams of the skirt and lining, leaving one side seam open down to the hip to allow for the zipper. Press seams open.

3. Mount the skirt on to the lining by tacking round the top seam with the seam allowances facing each other.

4. Cut a straight band of fabric 4 cm ($1\frac{5}{8}$ in) wide to match the peplum seam of the bodice exactly. Notch all seams that coincide with this seam on to the band.

5. Tack the skirt to the band so that it is flat at the front, becoming fuller towards the back in soft pleats.

6. Machine the waistband and zigzag the inside seam allowance.

7. Insert the zipper in the side opening by hand. Finish with hooks and eyes.

8. Press the hems of 1 cm ($\frac{3}{8}$ in) towards each other. Hand sew separately.

GEORGE I

The most beautiful feature of this period was the 'sack back', often featured in the paintings of Watteau. Since it is the back view of the bride that is seen the most in church, details here are important and the pleated train of this dress is the most stunning feature. The general silhouette is fairly representative of the period but I have simplified the construction to more contemporary standards giving a classical 'grand' wedding style perfectly suited to the twentieth century.

The dress itself has a fitted bodice with a square neckline back and front, and with all the seams, including the pointed waistline, piped in fine silk. The elbow-length sleeves and the neck are trimmed with frills of broderie anglaise or lace. The skirt has six panels and is fitted at the waist, flaring towards the hem. The pleated 'sack back' falling from the back neck is cut in one piece with the skirt so that the hem billows out into a beautiful full train.

A veil would hide the beauty of the train, so the headdress is based on a purchased Alice band covered with loops of frilled lace, broderie anglaise or flowers. These trimmings could be sewn on to a snood as a base. The bridesmaids could be dressed in this classical style but without the 'sack back' and using plain coloured silks or moiré. The silk piping could be in white to match the lace frills.

Suggested fabrics
Dress: slub silk, Thai silk, moiré, satin, taffeta, brocade.
Lining: rayon taffeta, bemburg.

Approximate fabric requirement for a size 12
Dress: 8 m ($8\frac{3}{4}$ yd).
Lining: 8 m ($8\frac{3}{4}$ yd).

Notions
One 40 cm (16 in) zipper, piping cord, lace or broderie anglaise frills, sewing thread.

Construction

Dress
1. Draft the pattern to full scale and add a 1 cm ($\frac{3}{8}$ in) seam allowance to all edges.

2. Cut out the pattern pieces in fabric and lining as shown on the pattern.

3. Mount all the bodice pieces, including the sleeves, on to the lining and zigzag the edges together.

4. Cut lengths of silk bias strip 3 cm ($1\frac{1}{8}$ in) wide. The total length required will be about 3 m (118 in), although not all in one piece.

5. Stitch piping cord into the folded strip using a zipper foot. Make the line of stitching as close to the enclosed cord as possible.

6. Insert piping across the top of the centre front bodice panel and press the seam allowances down on to the inside. Catch the seam allowances down to the inside lining by hand.

7. Stitch the shoulder seams of the bodice and press open.

8. Insert piping in the seam from the front waist to the back waist across the shoulder. Finish as in stage 6.

9. Edgestitch the front panel to the side front panels as close to the piping as possible. Repeat for the back (see p. 22, stages 7 and 8).

10. Sink stitch a double layer of ruffled lace or broderie anglaise round the outer neck edge. Use the drawing as a guide.

11. Mount the skirt panels on to the lining as in stage 3.

12. Stitch the three front panels together and press the seams open.

13. Stitch the front skirt to the front bodice, sandwiching the piping into the V-shaped seam (see stage 9). Press seams downwards.

14. Stitch the darts in the back skirt panels and press towards the centre.

15. Stitch the back bodice to the back skirt, inserting the piping as in stage 13.

16. Stitch left-hand side seams of dress, making sure that the piping at the waist matches at the sides. Press open.

17. Stitch right-hand side seam from the hip to the hem.

18. Press open the entire seam allowance of this side seam and insert a 40 cm (16 in) zipper by hand. This should go from the hip to the armhole. *The centre back should still be open.*

19. Stitch the two pieces of each sleeve together, pressing the seam allowances open.

20. Insert piping into the hem of the sleeves as for the bodice front (see stage 6).

21. Hand stitch circles of graded lace frills to the inside of the sleeves.

22. Tack the sleeves into the dress and machine. Bind or zigzag the seams, having trimmed them to 5 mm ($\frac{1}{4}$ in).

23. Stitch the longest centre back seam of the train and press seam open. This seam should preferably be on the selvage.

24. Tack the three pleats in position before stitching all four centre back pieces together in one seam, A to B, down to the waist only, stitching the sides of the pleated panel on to the skirt from the waist down.

25. You should now find that if the longest centre back seam is aligned with centre back seam A-B, the pleats should match the notches on the square back neck of the bodice, thus forming the long 'sack back' train.

26. Tack all thicknesses together at the top and bind the edges with bias-cut silk strip to simulate the piping on the rest of the bodice.

27. Turn the hem up 1.5 cm ($\frac{5}{8}$ in) and stitch to the lining by hand.

GEORGE II

Because the style of this period was stiffly corseted and heavily draped I have adapted the design to a more flowing gown, retaining some period details.

The front of the dress is fairly plain, but at the back the insertion of pleats into the seams from the waist down, creates a beautifully flared train. The only decorations on this dress are subtle details such as the silk piping in the seams down to the hip, finished with tiny bows and the piping around the deep scoop neck and the cuffs of the elbow-length sleeves. Both neck and sleeves are trimmed with delicate pleated ruffles of fine lace. Because there are no really elaborate details it is essential that the fabric of the dress is of the highest quality available. The fabric will 'make' the dress and even though white would look stunning, a pale colour such as oyster, cream or magnolia would be more unusual and would also adapt to a useful formal evening dress.

A wide brimmed hat would make the perfect headdress for this outfit. Although these can be bought ready-made, and at great expense, a far more practical idea would be to buy a simple untrimmed base and trim it lavishly with flowers of your own choice, matching the dress. In keeping with the period look, dress the bridesmaids in the same style, but without the added panels at the back. Use striped silk or striped Swiss voile for their dresses and if this is unavailable a flowered chintz or spotted voile would do. For headdresses use ribbon bows with streamers at the back of the head and even a few flowers.

Suggested fabrics
Dress: silk satin, Thai silk, moiré, silk taffeta, silk Ottoman.
Lining: rayon taffeta, bemburg.

Approximate fabric requirement for a size 12
Dress: 7 m ($7\frac{1}{2}$ yd).
Lining: 7 m ($7\frac{1}{2}$ yd).

Notions
One 50 cm (20 in) zipper, narrow silk ribbon, pleated lace ruffles, piping cord, seam binding (optional), sewing thread.

Construction

Dress
1. Draft the pattern to full scale and add a 1.5 cm ($\frac{5}{8}$ in) seam allowance to all edges.

2. Cut out all the pattern pieces in dress fabric. With the exception of the inserted pleat panels, duplicate all pieces in lining fabric.

3. Stitch the three front panels together inserting silk piping (see p. 22, stages 7 and 8) into the seams down to the position marked by the bow. Press seams open.

4. Stitch the side seams and press open.

5. Stitch one side of the pleat panel to the back side panels from the position of the bow down, matching the notches.

6. Stitch the centre back panels to the side back panels, inserting piping to the point where the pleat starts. Continue machining the centre back panels to the other side of the pleat panel.

7. Press the pleat inside so that it closes at the top and opens into a train at the hem.

8. Repeat the pleat insertion procedure on the centre back seam from the position of the bow down.

9. Insert a 50 cm (20 in) zipper into the centre back seam. This should be done by hand and should start above the position of the bow.

10. Stitch the shoulder seams and press open.

11. Make up a separate sleeveless lining. Leave a 50 cm (20 in) zipper opening on the centre back.

12. Tack silk piping to the outside of the neck edge with the corded edge of the piping pointing away from the neck.

13. Place the dress lining over the dress with right sides together. Tack round the neck edge and machine through all thicknesses using a zipper foot.

14. Clip the curves before turning the lining to the inside. Press the neck edge.

15. Tack the lining to the dress at the armholes.

16. Hand stitch the zipper opening of the lining 5 mm ($\frac{1}{4}$ in) from each side of the zipper teeth.

17. Machine the two-piece sleeves together and press seams open.

18. Repeat stage 17 for the sleeve linings.

19. Insert piping into the hems of the sleeves, sewing the lining in at the same time (see stages 12, 13 and 14).

20. Tack the sleeve head of the lining into the armhole and finish the raw edge by trimming the allowance to 5 mm ($\frac{1}{4}$ in) and binding or zigzagging.

21. Hand stitch a row of pleated, ruffled lace to the inside of the neck.

22. Repeat stage 21 for the outside of the sleeves, using a triple row if desired.

23. Make five small silk ribbon bows in the same fabric as the piping. Attach these to the base of the piping on the bodice seams.

24. Finally, turn the hems up 1 cm ($\frac{3}{8}$ in) to the inside and hand stitch.

EMPIRE EMPIRE

The devastation of the French Revolution brought not only a change in the politics of the time — it also created a strong change in the style of dress. The reaction against the stiff formality of the previous court gave way to a soft classical simplicity.

This high-waisted 'Empire' line has always been very flattering and has consequently been revived several times, adjusting well to different periods. This delicate feminine wedding dress must be made in a fine voile, muslin or chiffon to achieve the desired floaty effect of a light sheer coat over a dress. In fact, the ensemble is one piece, with an underskirt sewn into the dress. If wished, the front opening can be reversed to the back, since it is the back view that is seen during the wedding ceremony. The high bodice is lightly gathered on to a ribbon band, as are the slashed puffed sleeves. All edges are bound with narrow satin ribbon and caught together at intervals by tiny satin bows. If the overdress is to be white, one could use a pale pastel shade for the underskirt. In this case use the same shade for the ribbon bindings. For maximum effect the overdress should be cut longer than the underskirt so that it flows out around the whole garment.

The headdress should be a classical wreath of silk leaves, tiny flowers and pearls, and with a long silk tulle veil gathered into the wreath at the centre back. Dress the bridesmaids in the same style, but without the front opening. These dresses could be made in various pastel flower-printed voiles, chiffons, georgettes or cotton lawns, all with coloured underskirts. Flowered circlets would make suitable headresses.

Suggested fabrics
Overdress: spotted or striped Swiss voile, silk chiffon, muslin.
Underskirt: plain Jap silk.
Lining: Jap silk, rayon crepe de Chine.

Approximate fabric requirement for a size 12
Overdress: 5 m ($5\frac{1}{2}$ yd).
Underskirt: 3 m ($3\frac{1}{4}$ yd).
Lining: 1.5 m ($1\frac{3}{4}$ yd).

Notions

One 35 cm (14 in) lightweight zipper, narrow ribbon, sewing thread.

Construction

Overdress and underskirt

1. The underskirt of this dress is made less full enhancing the diaphanous effect of the overdress. Draft the pattern to full scale and cut separate patterns as shown. Add a 1 cm ($\frac{3}{8}$ in) seam allowance for all edges except the centre back; this should have a 1.5 cm ($\frac{5}{8}$ in) seam allowance for the insertion of the zipper.

2. Cut the bodice front and back in both fabric and lining. Mount the dress fabric on to the lining.

3. Bind the top of the bodice front and back with narrow ribbon.

4. Stitch the side seams using 5 mm ($\frac{1}{4}$ in) French seams.

5. Bind the armholes using 46 cm ($18\frac{1}{4}$ in) of ribbon, at the same time creating shoulder straps.

6. Bind the centre slits of the sleeves with narrow ribbon.

7. Stitch the side seams of the sleeves using 5 mm ($\frac{1}{4}$ in) French seams.

8. Gather the hem of the sleeves into 24 cm ($9\frac{1}{2}$ in) ribbon armbands.

9. Gather the sleeve head into the ribbon shoulder straps and stitch the sleeve into the armhole.

10. Topstitch a double row of ribbon down the centre front of the bodice to simulate a front opening.

11. Gather the bodice on to a 76 cm (30 in) band of narrow ribbon.

12. Bind the centre front openings of the overdress with narrow ribbon.

13. Stitch the side seams of the overdress using 5 mm ($\frac{1}{4}$ in) French seams.

14. Stitch a 1.5 cm ($\frac{5}{8}$ in) seam on the centre back selvage up to the notch marked for the zipper. Press seam open.

15. Repeat stages 13 and 14 for the lining.

16. Gather the tops of the underskirt and the overdress separately. Mount them together and topstitch the ribbon band of the bodice on to this making sure that all the side seams match.

17. Hand stitch the zipper into the centre back of the bodice, but only into the lining of the skirt. The gap in the overdress will not show due to its fullness.

18. Hand stitch a 2 cm ($\frac{7}{8}$ in) hem on the underskirt.

19. Machine roll the hem of the overdress.

20. Finish off the dress by attaching small ribbon bows at the shoulder, cuff and down the centre front of the overdress, catching the opening together at intervals as shown on the drawing.

George III

(1815)

The dress of this period is a further development of the Empire style, the silhouette is similar but decoration has been introduced in the form of frills, flounces and ruffles. The overall effect is that of a tiny jacket in a more heavy fabric over a lighter, long-sleeved dress with ruffles.

The high-waisted bodice with its stand-away collar and short puff sleeves should be made in a crisp fabric such as moiré or taffeta. The sheen of these fabrics will contrast with the matt white of the long tiered skirt and sleeves. For a stronger contrast make the bodice in a pale pastel colour. Broderie anglaise or a white patterned voile are most suitable for the layered skirt and the long sleeves. For convenience buy broderie anglaise that has already been frilled; alternatively, use a sheer patterned voile with broderie anglaise frills sewn to the various hemlines. An extremely attractive effect is achieved by using a coloured fabric for the underskirt (to match the bodice), so that it shows through the layers of white on top. The addition of more flounces at the hem and the use of matching pastel ribbons and bows will make a more elaborate and romantic dress, but this is left to individual taste.

The high collar makes a veil unnecessary; instead a cluster of silk flowers at the back of the head would be attractive.

Suggested fabrics
Bodice: moiré, taffeta, Thai silk, satin, Ottoman.
Dress: broderie anglaise, striped, spotted or flowered Swiss voile.
Lining: rayon taffeta, bemburg.

Approximate fabric requirement for a size 12
Bodice and sleeves: 2 m (2¼ yd).
Dress: 1½ m (1¾ yd).
Lining: 2 m (2¼ yd).

Notions
One 28 cm (11 in) zipper, four buttons, rouleau loops, seam binding, broderie anglaise frills, interfacing, sewing thread.

Construction

Bodice and dress

1. Draft the pattern to full scale and add a 1.5 cm ($\frac{5}{8}$ in) seam allowance to all edges of the bodice, collar, puff sleeves and facing.

2. Add a 1 cm ($\frac{3}{8}$ in) seam allowance to all edges of the skirt, underskirt and undersleeves. These should all have 5 mm ($\frac{1}{4}$ in) French seams.

3. Mount the bodice fronts and back on to lining fabric.

4. Stitch shoulder darts and press.

5. Stitch the shoulder and side seams, leaving the right-hand side seam open from the notch marked to allow for a 28 cm (11 in) zipper. Press the seams open and finish by zigzagging the edges.

6. Stitch the bust darts and press towards the centre.

7. Stitch the outer collar to the neckline of the bodice. Clip the curves and press open. If using a fine fabric interface the collar and front facing (which should have its inner edge zigzagged).

8. Stitch the inner collar to the facing, matching the notch with the shoulder line on the facing. Clip the curves and press open.

9. Tack the facing and inner collar to the outside of the bodice, right sides together. Machine up the fronts and round the top of the collar. Trim the seams and turn the facing and inner collar to the inside of the garment, pressing the edge firmly.

10. Hand stitch the inside neck edge of the inner collar, attaching it to the back neck seam allowance.

11. Add the front fastening here. Either machined buttonholes and buttons or rouleau loops and fabric-covered buttons would be suitable. Once these have been worked, overlap the fronts matching the centre fronts and tack together.

12. Stitch the side seams of the puff sleeves and press open.

13. Gather the lower edge of the sleeve into a narrow folded band as shown on the pattern.

14. Gather the top of the sleeve head and tack it into the armhole of the jacket.

15. Stitch the narrow contrast sleeves together using 5 mm ($\frac{1}{4}$ in) French seams. Finish the bottoms of these sleeves with ruffles of lace or broderie anglaise.

16. Tack the narrow sleeves with the puff sleeves inside the armholes of the bodice. Machine through all thicknesses and trim the seam to 5 mm ($\frac{1}{4}$ in). Finish off by binding or zigzagging.

17. Stitch the side seams of the underskirt, leaving the right-hand seam open above the notch for the zipper.

18. Stitch graded borders of frilled broderie anglaise to the line marked on the pattern. The number of layers used is entirely up to the individual.

19. Stitch the side seams of the overskirt using 5 mm ($\frac{1}{4}$ in) French seams and leaving the right-hand seam open above the notch for the zipper.

20. Mount the two skirts together at the top, making sure that the top skirt just covers the first seam of the layers underneath.

21. Gather the skirts on to the bodice matching the centre fronts, side seams and centre backs. Make sure that the fullness at the front starts at the notch marked by the bust dart so that the centre front area is flat.

22. Bind the seam allowances together on the inside of the bodice.

23. Insert the zipper by machine. Stitch it into the bodice, but then only into the underskirt so that the fullness of the overskirt hides the zipper.

24. Turn up the hem of the lining so that it is just visible below the last decorative frill.

GEORGE IV

By 1827 the waist had dropped to a more natural level with the emphasis being on width across the shoulders balanced by elaborate headdresses or hats. The relatively simple design of this dress relies on the lavish use of frills around the neck and the delicate appliqué decoration.

The choice of fabric is important and a sheer patterned fabric over a pale pastel lining would be the most effective combination for both a wedding dress and an evening gown. The fitted bodice has a wide square neck trimmed with a deep flounce of frilled broderie anglaise or lace. A double or even a triple frill can be used, according to individual taste. The full puff sleeves are unlined and gathered into a deep cuff which is decorated in the same way as the shaped waistband. Ready-made appliqués are available for this decoration; alternatively, buy 25 cm ($9\frac{7}{8}$ in) of heavy guipure lace, cut out the motifs and hand sew them to the fabric. This will give the effect of expensive hand embroidery! The skirt is in four panels, narrow on the hips and flaring out to a full hem. Ideally the skirt should be cut slightly longer at the back so that it forms a flattering train (the lining should remain floor length).

For the headdress use a triple ruffle of lace (to match the collar) attached to a wired Alice band. If worn far back on the head this can be secured with a plastic hair comb. The tulle veil is gathered to the inside of the Alice band. The bridesmaids should wear dresses of the same shape in striped voile but without the lavish trimming and train.

Suggested fabrics

Dress: white striped, spotted or flowered Swiss voile, broderie anglaise, organza.
Lining: Jap silk, rayon crepe de Chine.

Approximate fabric requirement for a size 12

Dress: 6.75 m ($7\frac{1}{2}$ yd).
Lining: 6.75 m ($7\frac{1}{2}$ yd).

Notions

One 50 cm (20 in) zipper, interfacing, purchased appliqué for waistband broderie anglaise or lace ruffles, sewing thread.

Construction

Dress

1. Draft the pattern to full scale and add a seam allowance of 1.5 cm ($\frac{5}{8}$ in) to the bodice front, bodice back and the waistband. Add an allowance of 3 cm ($1\frac{1}{8}$ in) to the centre back seam for the insertion of the zipper.

2. Add a 1 cm ($\frac{3}{8}$ in) seam allowance on the puff sleeve, cuff and skirt lining (except centre back seam, see above). These will have 5 mm ($\frac{1}{4}$ in) French seams.

3. Mount the bodice front, back and the waistbands on to the lining fabric. If the waistband is to support embroidery it may be advisable to use interfacing here.

4. Stitch the bust darts and press towards the centre.

5. Stitch the back darts and press towards the centre.

6. If using an embroidered appliqué for the waistband, mount it at this stage while the pattern pieces are still flat.

7. Stitch the shoulder seams and press open.

8. Press the 1.5 cm ($\frac{5}{8}$ in) seam allowance of the square neck to the outside. This will be covered by the deep lace frills.

9. Stitch the side seams of the bodice and press open.

10. Stitch the side seams of the waistband and press open.

11. Pin the top of the waistband to the bottom of the bodice, matching the side seams and centre fronts. Tack. Machine together pressing the seam allowances down. Topstitch 5 mm ($\frac{1}{4}$ in) in from the edge of the waistband.

12. Stitch the side seams of the sleeves using 5 mm ($\frac{1}{4}$ in) French seams.

13. Assemble the sleeves as for the previous chapter (see p. 54, stages 12, 13 and 14). Remember to mount the cuff on to the lining before applying the appliqué and topstitch just as on the waistband (see stage 11).

14. Stitch the sleeves into the bodice with the fullness coming at the top of the shoulder.

15. Trim the armhole seam allowance to 5 mm ($\frac{1}{4}$ in) and zigzag the edges together.

16. Lay the deepest layer of ruffles on top of the neck and mitre at the corners.

17. Build up the layers of ruffles by topstitching them over the pressed out seam allowance. Do not stitch them down at the centre back since they will help to conceal the zipper.

18. Stitch the skirt panels together using 5 mm ($\frac{1}{4}$ in) French seams for all but the centre back seam. Allow a 3 cm ($1\frac{1}{8}$ in) seam here and leave open above the notch to allow for the 50 cm (20 in) zipper.

19. Repeat stage 18 for the lining.

20. Pin the skirt on to the waistband, being careful to match the centre front 'V' and the side seams. Tack.

21. Machine this seam, zigzag the allowance and press upwards. Topstitch as for the top of the waistband (see stage 11).

22. The zipper can be machined into the bodice, but it is advisable to insert the skirt section by hand since the seam is not on the straight grain.

23. The lining can be hemmed by turning up 5 mm ($\frac{1}{4}$ in) and edgestitching. The outer skirt, however, must be machine or hand rolled.

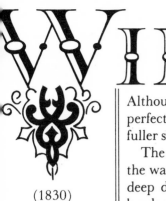

WILLIAM IV

(1830)

Although we have only moved on three years since George IV, this period is perfect for the modern bride and we can adapt the fuller skirt and even fuller sleeves into another pretty wedding or evening dress.

The tight-waisted bodice has a deep V-neck, falling from the shoulder to the waist. This bodice is filled in white broderie anglaise and edged with a deep double ruffle of the same fabric. The high neck is also edged with broderie anglaise frills. The very full sleeves are gathered tightly into a cuff that matches the collar. The billowing skirt is cut in four flared panels and gathered into the waist which is accentuated by a belt made in the same fabric as the dress. In order to do without the petticoats that traditionally hold the hem out, the skirt must be stiffened. Alternatively, a frill of broderie anglaise sewn inside the hem would be most attractive. This would just show at the base of the skirt, giving the illusion of many petticoats underneath. Again, fabric choice is important to give this dress the sense of occasion it deserves. The most suitable fabric for the dress would be one with a sheen or surface texture or, as the bodice is predominantly white, a very pale pastel shade could be used.

Use a wreath of tiny roses with ribbon streamers at the back for the headdress and, if wished, attach a veil to the back. The bridesmaids could wear ankle-length dresses in the same style but made in a delicate floral printed cotton lawn.

Suggested fabrics
Bodice: broderie anglaise.
Dress: silk paper taffeta, moiré, satin, white cotton piqué.
Lining: rayon taffeta, bemburg.

Approximate fabric requirement for a size 12
Bodice panel, collar and cuffs: 1.5 m ($1\frac{3}{4}$ yd).
Dress: 5 m ($5\frac{1}{2}$ yd).
Lining: 5 m ($5\frac{1}{2}$ yd).

Notions
One 55 cm (22 in) zipper, broderie anglaise frills, narrow ribbon, interfacing, sewing thread.

Construction

Bodice and dress
1. Draft the pattern to full scale and add a 1.5 cm ($\frac{5}{8}$ in) seam allowance to all edges except the centre back. Allow 3 cm ($1\frac{1}{8}$ in) here for the insertion of a 55 cm (22 in) zip.

2. Cut out the centre front bodice panel, collar, cuffs and centre back panel in broderie anglaise.

3. The remaining pattern pieces should be cut in the chosen fabric.

4. Cut out the lining, omitting the broderie anglaise sections.

5. Stitch the front side bodice panels together, trim the seams and press open.

6. Repeat stage 5 for the lining.

7. Stitch the broderie anglaise front panel in, carefully matching the notches. Press away from the centre front.

8. Repeat stages 5, 6 and 7 for the back bodice and lining.

9. Stitch the shoulder seams, trim to 1 cm ($\frac{3}{8}$ in) and press open.

10. Stiffen the collar with white interfacing and bag out up the centre backs and along the top. Press the edges and add a double row of broderie anglaise frills round the top edge.

11. Stitch the collar to the neck opening, trim the allowance to 5 mm ($\frac{1}{4}$ in) and zigzag the edges together on the inside.

12. Open out the bodice flat and tack the wide broderie anglaise frill along the V-shaped front and back seams. Place a length of narrow baby ribbon over the edge and topstitch down.

13. Stitch the side seams of the sleeves and press open.

14. Pin the sleeves into the armholes, starting at the side seams and working up to the notches. Begin pleating gently until you reach the shoulder seam. Tack and machine. Trim the seam to 1 cm ($\frac{3}{8}$ in).

15. Stitch the side seams of the lining, press open and pin into the bodice round the armhole. Tack and zigzag together with the bodice.

16. Fold the edge of the lining inside the edge of the V-shaped seam, back and front. Hand stitch using the lower row of ribbon topstitching as a guide.

17. Make up the cuffs in broderie anglaise following the procedure used for the collar in stage 11.

18. Sew in the cuffs and finish off as for the collar in stage 11.

19. Stitch the four skirt panels together leaving the seam open above the notch marked on the centre back for the zipper. Press open.

20. Repeat stage 19 for the lining.

21. Mount the lining on to the skirt with wrong sides together.

22. Match the side seams, centre front seams and centre back seams of the skirt to the bodice and gently gather the rest of the skirt into the waist seam.

23. Stitch through to the bodice (not the bodice lining) and press seam upwards.

24. Fold in the waist seam of the lining and hand stitch the seam leaving a small gap at the centre back for the zipper.

25. Press the seam allowance of the centre back open and insert the zipper by hand.

26. Hand stitch the lining 5 mm ($\frac{1}{4}$ in) away from the zipper teeth.

27. Turn up the hems 2 cm ($\frac{7}{8}$ in) to the inside and hand stitch.

EARLY VICTORIAN

(1843)

Although the width of the shoulder is still emphasized in this period, the general look is becoming more austere and tailored. For contemporary purposes I have softened the image with a triple-layered lace sleeve and deep pleated edgings.

The fitted bodice has a wide V-shaped neck, bordered with three rows of pleats. This line is echoed by the V-shaped waist seam, accentuated by piping. The full skirt is pleated into the waist, becoming more full towards the centre back, and billowing out at the hem with a triple row of horizontally stitched pleats. The beauty of this dress relies on the use of a special fabric, preferably one with a sheen on it, so that the depth of light is caught by the pleats, contrasting with the delicate nature of the lace frills around the arm.

The dress is complemented by an extravagant headdress, such as a cluster of silk roses and large ribbon loops. The full silk tulle veil should be gathered into the centre of this at the back of the head. In keeping with the style of this period, dress the bridesmaids in high-necked Victorian-style dresses, perhaps with discreet lace ruffles round the neck and cuffs. The most suitable fabric would be one with a small, dark flowered print.

Suggested fabrics

Dress: white paper taffeta, moiré, satin.
Lining: rayon taffeta, bemburg.

Approximate fabric requirement for a size 12

Dress: 6.5 m (7 yd).
Lining: 6.5 m (7 yd).

Notions

One 55 cm (22 in) zipper, antique or purchased lace ruffles for the cuffs, seam binding, piping cord, sewing thread.

Construction

Dress

1. Draft the pattern to full scale and cut out the front bodice section and trace off the three pleated areas. Double these in width and add a 2 cm ($\frac{7}{8}$ in) seam allowance on each. You will notice that the bodice fronts and backs are in two sections and not three (the heavy black line denotes centre front and centre back panels). The folded pleats are bias cut strips folded in half and overlapped by 2 cm ($\frac{7}{8}$ in) so that no stitching shows.

2. Repeat stage 1 for the back bodice.

65

3. Open up the fold lines of the sleeves by 4 cm ($1\frac{5}{8}$ in) each. When they are stitched back you will have 2 x 2 cm ($\frac{7}{8}$ x $\frac{7}{8}$ in) pin tucks along the hem of each sleeve.

4. Repeat stage 3 for the hem of the dress.

5. Add a 1.5 cm ($\frac{5}{8}$ in) seam allowance to all edges except the centre back. Allow 3 cm ($1\frac{1}{8}$ in) here for the insertion of the 55 cm (22 in) zipper.

6. Having cut out the front panel use tailors' chalk to mark lines A, B and C as a guide for the pleats.

7. Repeat stage 6 for the back bodice.

8. Stitch the front bodice panel to the side panels and press seams open.

9. Repeat stage 8 for the back bodice.

10. Stitch the side seams and press open.

11. Stitch the shoulder seams and press open.

12. Stitch the sleeve seams and press open.

13. Tack the sleeves into the armholes since their construction is not as simple as contemporary sleeve heads.

14. Join the six bias cut strips for each side at the shoulder seams. Fold them all in half.

15. Starting with strip A, lay them along the chalked line A with the folded edge pointing downwards and topstitch down 5 mm ($\frac{1}{4}$ in) from the raw edge.

16. Lay strip B along guideline B so that the folded edge overlaps the stitching on strip A. Topstitch down.

17. Repeat stage 16 for strip C.

18. Stitch the centre fronts catching the pleats and making sure that they make a perfect chevron at the front.

19. Stitch the six lining pieces of the bodice together, pressing all the seams flat as you go.

20. Place the lining on top of the bodice, right sides together and machine round the neckline. Clip the curves and snip right into the 'V', which should be double stitched.

21. Turn the lining to the inside of the bodice and press firmly.

22. Attach the lining to the bodice at the armhole by binding or zigzagging.

23. Stitch the four panels of the skirt together making sure that the pleats worked in stage 4 all match at the seams. Stitch only up to the notch marked for the zipper in the centre back seam.

24. Repeat stage 23 for the lining and mount both skirt and lining.

25. Insert silk piping (see p. 22, stages 5 to 8) along the waist seam of the bodice, pressing the seam allowances inwards and upwards so that the piping is on the very edge.

26. Pin the pleats away from the centre front to coincide with the notches on the bodice. These must be marked with tailor's tacks since the seam allowance is no longer visible.

27. Place the bodice over the skirt with the centre front 'V' over-lapping on to the centre front seam. Tack in position.

28. Using a zipper foot sink stitch the bodice on to the skirt and lining keeping the stitching as close to the piping as possible.

29. Hand stitch the bodice lining to the waist seam from the inside.

30. Insert the zipper by hand and then stitch the lining to its edge.

31. Turn the two hems up by hand.

32. Finally, if you are lucky enough to find any good lace in a market or antique shop, use this for the cuffs. If not, buy the finest frilled lace and attach three graduated layers to the inside of the short sleeve.

PRE-RAPHAELITE

Between 1850 and 1890 skirts developed to the full crinoline with the back becoming draped into a bustle — both styles being totally unsuitable for contemporary use. However, during the 1890s, whilst the majority of the population were strictly corseted, there was the growth of a freer aesthetic movement called Art Nouveau. Although this was a minority movement, the loose flowing styles with elaborate details were not only beautiful in their time, but are perfect for wear in the twentieth century. A Pre-Raphaelite revival occurred in the 1960s and was much abused, but if used with constraint and careful attention to detail and fabric, this style can be very flattering and is easily adaptable for evening wear.

This design has a square-necked yoke which can be made more elaborate by quilting, embroidery and beading with pearls and sequins. The yoke, cuffs and hem are made with a rich patterned brocade to offset the large areas of plain fabric and all are further enhanced by the use of silk piping. The body of the dress consists of four flared panels with a V-shaped area of pin tucks over the bust and also at the back, forming a train. The very full sleeves are gathered on to the shoulder and emphasized by long silk cords trimmed with silk leaves and pearls.

For this dress, the wider the fabric the better, since the style relies on a neat construction at the top going down to the billowing hem at the base. Furnishing fabric such as linen, artificial slub silk or Ottoman would all be ideal for the main body of the dress. As only a relatively small amount of brocade is needed for the yoke, cuffs and hem, it will be possible to use a more luxurious fabric. The dress need not be lined unless a more silky fabric is used for the main body.

The headdress is a simple wreath of matching leaves and pearls. The bridesmaids should be dressed in the same style but without the silk cords and embroidery. Their dresses could be made in an Art Nouveau style printed cotton lawn such as a Liberty print.

Suggested fabrics

Yoke, cuffs and hem: brocade, damask, cloque.
Dress: silk shantung, Thai silk, Jap silk, taffeta.
Lining: Jap silk, rayon crepe de Chine.

Approximate fabric requirement for a size 12

Yoke, cuffs and hem: 1.5 m ($1\frac{1}{2}$ yd).
Dress: 6 m ($6\frac{1}{2}$ yd).

Notions

One 30 cm (12 in) zipper, piping cord, silk cords, leaves and pearls, sewing thread.

Construction

Dress

1. Draft the pattern to full scale and cut out the yoke, cuffs and hem facing in the patterned fabric adding a 1 cm ($\frac{3}{8}$ in) seam allowance to all edges.

2. Cut out the main body of the dress and sleeves in plain fabric. Add a 1.5 cm ($1\frac{5}{8}$ in) seam allowance to all edges except the centre back. Allow 3 cm ($1\frac{1}{8}$ in) here for the insertion of a 30 cm (12 in) zipper.

3. Mark the position of the pin tucks using tailors' chalk and tack in place.

4. Machine the pin tucks. When doing this it is important to start from the centre and work outwards, pressing each one as you go. By doing this one avoids one incorrect pin tuck spoiling all the others.

5. Press all the pin tucks away from the centre so that they radiate out. Work a line of stay stitching round the yoke edge to keep the whole neckline in place.

6. Cut linings for the yoke and cuffs. Stitch the shoulder seams of the lining and the dress fabric.

7. Stitch silk piping round the square neck using the method described on p.42, stages 4, 5 and 6. Place the yoke lining on top of the patterned yoke and its piping. Tack in place and machine round the square neck using the zipper foot, working as close to the piping as possible.

8. Clip the corners and turn the yoke lining to the inside. Press so that the piping shows only round the square neck edge.

9. Insert piping into the lower edges of the front and back yoke using the zipper foot.

10. Press the seam allowances of the lower edges of the yokes upwards and inwards so that the piping shows on the actual edge.

11. If the dress is to be lined, work pin tucks in the lining (see stages 3, 4 and 5).

12. Stitch the centre front seam of the dress and press open.

13. Stitch the centre back seam of the dress up to the notch marked for the zipper. Press open.

14. Stitch the side seams of the dress and press open.

15. Lay the dress yoke on top of the pin tucks, back and front, and sink stitch the yokes to the main body of the garment. Use the zipper foot so that the stitching is hidden by the piping.

16. Stitch together all four pieces of the brocade hem, trim and press open.

17. If wished insert silk piping into the upper edge of the hem. Press the seam allowance downwards with the piping showing on the upper edge.

18. Stitch the border to the inside edge of the hem, press it to the right side and edgestitch down as close to the piping as possible and through to the skirt. The hem of the lining is worked separately.

EDWARDIAN

(1908)

Having bypassed the heavily corseted rigidity of the early Edwardian period, we move into a softer, more feminine silhouette used mostly for the summer wear of the period. The styles of this period relied on the use of fine lawns which were delicately detailed by the use of pin tucking, lace insertion and embroidery. I have attempted to create this image by the simple use of lace, frills and finely pleated chiffon or voile.

The design has a circular yoke filled in with a very fine embroidered lace — antique lace bought from a market or antique shop would be ideal. Although white would be the obvious choice for a wedding dress, cream would be more subtle and would adapt to a stunning evening dress for later use. If using cream fabric for the main body of the dress and only white lace is available, dip the lace in cold tea which will 'discolour' it. The high neck, cuffs and bands around the skirt are of narrow lace with the neck yoke and cuffs trimmed with frilled lace edging. The lower bodice and hip yoke should be in matching silk or satin. The dress is belted by a silk or satin ruched cummerbund. Alternatively use a wide silk satin sash tied in a bow at the back. Use pleated silk chiffon or voile for the sleeves and layered skirt.

A cluster of silk roses with a narrow tulle veil gathered into the back would make a suitable headdress. Alternatively wear a large brimmed hat laden with flowers, feathers and veiling. Dress the bridesmaids in a similar style using fewer lace frills.

Suggested fabrics

Yoke: fine embroidered lace or voile.
Bodice and hip yoke: silk or satin.
Sleeves and skirt: pleated silk chiffon or voile.

Approximate fabric requirement for a size 12

Pleating: 9 m ($9\frac{3}{4}$ yd) fabric to be pleated.
Lace yoke: 0.75 m ($\frac{7}{8}$ yd).
Lower bodice and hip yoke: 2 m ($2\frac{1}{4}$ yd).
Lining: 5 m ($5\frac{1}{2}$ yd).

Notions

One 40 cm (16 in) zipper, 5.75 m ($6\frac{1}{4}$ yd) 5 cm (2 in) wide lace bands, 3 m ($3\frac{1}{4}$ yd) lace frills, pearl ball buttons or silk-covered ball buttons for neck and yoke, sewing thread.

73

Construction

Dress

1. Draft the pattern to full scale adding a 1 cm ($\frac{3}{8}$ in) seam allowance to all edges except the centre back of the lower bodice and back hip yoke which should have a 3 cm ($1\frac{1}{8}$ in) seam allowance for the insertion of the zipper.

2. Stitch the front and back darts of the satin bodice, top and bottom sections. Press towards the centre front and centre back.

3. Repeat stages 1 and 2 in lining fabric.

4. Stitch shoulder seams of the lace yoke, finishing with 5 mm ($\frac{1}{4}$ in) French seams.

5. Stitch the waist seams of the bodices. Press open.

6. Repeat stage 5 for the lining.

7. Stitch the side seams of the outer bodice and lining. Press open.

8. Stitch the three bands of lace into separate circles. Stitch the three tiers of pleated chiffon into three separate circles, finishing with 5 mm ($\frac{1}{4}$ in) French seams.

9. Tack the top yoke line and the hip yoke line of the bodice together with right sides facing outside. (This will leave the centre backs open.)

10. Stitch the lace yoke to the top edge of the bodice, matching the notches and with seam allowances on the right side.

11. Using a 5 mm ($\frac{1}{4}$ in) French seam, stitch the inside seams of the pleated sleeves on the straight grain, leaving a 6 cm ($2\frac{1}{2}$ in) opening at the cuff. Hand roll and hand stitch this opening to finish.

12. Close up the pleats at the sleeve head so that they fit the armhole formed by the bodice and yoke.

13. Tack the sleeves in, machine and finish off on the inside using a narrow zigzag stitch.

14. Topstitch the layers of ruffles round the lace yoke, covering the raw seam allowances underneath.

15. Stitch the straight band of lace, 36 cm ($14\frac{1}{4}$ in) in length, to the neck with the seam allowance on the right side for the collar. Cover this edge with a ruffle of lace and repeat for the top edge of the collar. (If the lace band is very fine it should be mounted on to net to stiffen it.)

16. The centre back of the yoke and collar can be fastened using tiny rouleau loops and covered buttons, or pearls and hand-worked chain loops.

17. Insert the 40 cm (16 in) zipper into the satin bodice by hand.

18. Work the cuffs as for the neck in stages 15 and 16.

19. Gather the pleated sleeves into the made-up cuff and zigzag the 5 mm ($\frac{1}{4}$ in) seam allowances together on the inside.

20. Fasten the cuffs as in stage 16.

21. Tack the first band of lace to the bottom of the yoke overlapping the satin yoke and lining by 1 cm ($\frac{3}{8}$ in).

22. Machine the first tier of pleats flat and repeat stage 21.

23. Machine a narrow row of zigzag stitch at the edge of the lace.

24. Trim the seam allowance from the inside, right up to the edge of the zigzag stitching.

25. Repeat stages 21 to 24 for the second tier of pleating.

26. On the bottom edge of the second tier of pleating, press out the pleats and zigzag on a 3 m ($3\frac{1}{4}$ yd) band of lace border. Trim as in stage 24.

27. Stitch a 3 m ($3\frac{1}{4}$ yd) band of closed pleats on the bottom edge of the lace, trimming the seam allowance on the inside of the pleated fabric down to the zigzag stitching.

28. Press out the hem of the third tier and machine the edge into a tight rolled hem so that it flutes out at the bottom.

29. Make up the skirt pattern for the lining. Hand stitch it into the waist.

30. If a cummerbund sash is desired, cut a 30 cm (12 in) strip of satin on the bias to the required waist measurement, ruche it at the back and finish with hooks and eyes.

THE TWENTIES

From the grandeur of the Edwardian period we move to the Twenties, bypassing the uncertain and disturbing years of the First World War that nevertheless completely changed the role of women in society and consequently their looks. Suddenly corsets were abandoned and legs revealed in a tubular 'unstructured' look completely different to the style typical of the pre-war period.

The design featured here is quite adaptable to current fashion and if made in a plain jersey fabric it would suit almost any occasion. However, for a wedding dress use the most luxurious fabrics available. Silk satin would be suitable for the entire outfit or a combination of silk satin for the bodice and chiffon or organdie for the skirt could be used. Use either beaded braid or delicate lace edging as decoration. The dress has a hip-length bodice with a side fastening and a square neck. The knee-length wrap-over skirt has a 'waterfall' frill edging, a feature which is repeated on the cuffs.

For the headdress use a bandeau of small silk flowers with a circular veil matching the detail of the skirt. Dress the bridesmaids in dresses of a similar style but without the 'waterfall' frill and with less lavish trimming.

Suggested fabrics
Dress: silk satin, fine wool crepe, crepe de Chine, silk jersey, fine rayon jersey, chiffon, organdie.
Lining: Jap silk, bemberg.

Approximate fabric requirement for a size 12
Dress: 4 m ($4\frac{1}{2}$ yd).
Lining: 3 m ($3\frac{1}{4}$ yd).

Notions
Approximately 32 1cm ($\frac{3}{8}$ in) fabric-covered buttons, 2 m ($2\frac{1}{4}$ yd) beaded braid or lace edging, sewing thread

Construction
Dress

1. Draft the pattern to full scale adding a 1 cm ($\frac{3}{8}$ in) seam allowance to all edges.

2. Stitch the bust and shoulder darts of both bodice and lining. Press the darts flat.

3. Stitch the shoulder and side seams of both bodice and lining. Press the seams open.

4. Cut strips of bias fabric 2 cm ($\frac{5}{8}$ in) wide to make rouleau loops which should each be 3 cm ($1\frac{1}{8}$ in) in length.

5. Lay the bodice lining over the bodice, right sides together.

6. Tack round the neck edge, sandwiching the loops between the two layers down the front of the wrap-over.

7. Machine round the neck edge, clip the corners and turn the lining to the inside of the bodice.

8. Press the edges and tack the lining to the armhole of the bodice.

9. Tack the braid or lace up the front of the side opening and round the neck. Mitre at the corners.

10. Machine or hand stitch the trimming down on both edges.

11. Stitch the two sleeve pieces, leaving an 8 cm ($3\frac{1}{4}$ in) gap as shown on the pattern.

12. Press the seams open and zigzag the raw edges.

13. Hand stitch the rouleau loops to the sleeve opening as in stages 6 and 7.

14. Stitch the circular cuff round the edge and opening using a tiny zigzag stitch to finish the edges.

15. Stitch the cuff on to the sleeve with the seam allowances on the outside. Press the allowances upwards.

16. Hand stitch the braid or lace round the base of the sleeve, covering the seam allowances.

17. Tack the sleeves into the armholes of the bodice. Machine in and either bind the armhole seam or finish with a zigzag stitch.

18. Wrap the bodice over so that the centre front of the under panel meets the centre front of the over panel on the hip line.

19. Stitch the overlaps together along the hip line.

20. Hand sew a press stud to the under-wrap at the neck line to fasten at the centre front.

21. Stitch a minute zigzag around the curve of the over skirt, 1 cm ($\frac{3}{8}$ in) from the edge. Cut off the extra fabric round the edge right up to the edge of the zigzag.

22. Stitch the four panels of the skirt together inserting the curved panel into the right-hand side seam. Use 5 mm ($\frac{1}{4}$ in) French seams if the fabric is a sheer one. Press seams, making sure that the bottom edge starts 1 cm ($\frac{3}{8}$ in) up from the bottom of the other skirt panels to allow for the hem.

23. Stitch the four panels of the lining and press the seams open.

24. Tack the skirt and lining together round the hip line, making sure to match the seams and the fluted panel notches to those on the hip line of the bodice.

25. Tack the skirt to the bodice and machine. Finish the seam allowances using a zigzag stitch.

26. Zigzag the hem of the skirt as in stage 21. Turn up the lining 1 cm ($\frac{3}{8}$ in) and hand stitch.

Notes on the lay-out guide

All lay-outs are for fabric 90 cm (36 in) wide, except number 14 (Early Victorian) which needs fabric 115 cm (45 in) wide.

Patterns numbers 5, 7, 10, 12, 13, 14, 15 and 17:

If you are making up these patterns in one-way fabric, you should cut along the fold line and turn the lower piece of fabric so that it faces the same way as the top one.

(The other lay-outs are all arranged to be suitable for one-way fabrics. If you are making up these patterns using two-way fabric, you may be able to find more economical ways of laying out the pieces by turning some of them round.)

Patterns numbers 4 and 16 (Reformation and Edwardian):

Lay-outs are given for pieces in plain fabric only. The arrangement of the pleated pieces will depend on how wide your fabric is after it has been pleated. For instructions on cutting out pleated fabric, see page 26, points 3, 4 and 5.